Without Masks, Without Fear

RUBÍ ASTRÒLOGAS

The act of revealing who you are in a world that still punishes difference.

Alina A. Rubi

Published independently.

Author: Alina A. Rubí

Editing: Angeline Rubí

Contact: rubiediciones29@gmail.com

Dedication

To those who have had to hide a part of themselves just to survive.

To those who love differently, dream in unusual ways, dress without asking permission, believe without proof, or think outside the mold.

To those who have been called "too much," "too little," "wrong," or "dangerous" simply for being authentic.

This book is for you.

Because living out loud is not rebellion—

it is resistance, truth, and an act of self-love.

Introduction

There are moments in life when you look in the mirror and don't recognize yourself. Not because his face has changed, but because he has been blurring inside. By dint of pleasing, of fitting in, of lowering one's voice or feigning enthusiasm where there was only silence. This book was born from there: from the fatigue of holding a version of oneself that has no roots, only makeup. It is born of the deep desire to say enough. Enough fear. Enough of disguises. Enough of living apologizing for being different, intense, emotional, rebellious, free.

This is not a book that seeks to please you. It was not written to win everyone's applause, nor to adorn shelves with sweet and empty phrases. This book makes uncomfortable what hurts and embrace what has been ignored. It comes to say what we often keep quiet for fear of judgment, of abandonment, of being left alone in the middle of a system that punishes difference. But he also comes to celebrate. To honor every part of you that has survived hidden. To recognize that, despite the noise outside, your voice is still alive. Maybe broken, maybe short, but intact in truth.

Here you will not find instructions to be happy or promises of express success. You're going to find uncomfortable truths, yes. But also refuge. You're going to find stories that might look like yours, even though you thought you were the only one. You will find words that do not seek to correct you, but to remind you that you are not wrong. That you are not alone. That you are not crazy, or defective, or exaggerated. That being you – with your lights, your shadows, your slow processes, and your emotions on the surface – is an act of love. And also of resistance.

This book is an open letter to those who have been silenced for having a different voice, a different skin, a different orientation, a story that does not enter the margins of what others call "normal". It is for those who do not fit, those who do not want to obey, those who doubt everything and still continue walking. It's for people who have learned to live in armor but dream of getting emotionally naked and still having peace.

Perfection is not required here. You don't have to be cured to belong. You don't have to have answers to stay. All you need is something you already have: the intention to be you. Even if you don't always know how. Even if your voice still trembles. Even if there are days when you feel like you're going backwards. This book is not going to judge you. This book is not going to ask you to be anything else. This book is here to accompany you as you recover, as you rearm, as you remember everything that at some point you were forced to forget.

So, if you're tired of pretending, if you're tired of pleasing, if you can't stand a life that doesn't look like you anymore... This is your place. You don't have to prove anything here. Just sit down, breathe, and start reading. Or perhaps, start listening to you.

Because, even if you don’t believe it, this book already knows you.

It has been waiting for you.

And now that you’re here, we can start over.

Without masks.

Without permission.

And, above all, without fear.

The Echo of Silence and the Call to Authenticity

There is a moment in life when one stops turning a deaf ear and begins to hear the echo of one's own silence. Not the silence of others, not the uncomfortable one you feel when no one answers a message, but the silence that settles inside, like a guest who did not ask permission but came to stay. That silence is not always kind; sometimes he screams. It screams what one has been silent about for years, what one swallowed to please, to fit in, to avoid the family drama or the strange look of the boss. It is a silence with its own personality, with the voice of conscience, fear and also the courage that still does not dare to go on stage.

Psychology calls it cognitive dissonance: that uncomfortable clash between what one does and what one is. But in practice it feels more like living in an itchy costume. One smiles while inside one wonders if someone else will notice that the suit does not fit, that the sleeves are from another story and the buttons no longer close. People get used to living like this, disguised as what others expect, until one day there is no longer room to breathe. And that's when the echo becomes unbearable. Not because it's loud, but because it can no longer be ignored.

Then the call comes—not from your cell phone, but from your soul. A voice that doesn't make a sound but pushes. It has no number, yet it insists. It doesn't appear with trumpets or neon lights; instead, it shows up as Sunday night anxiety or that inexplicable sadness right after doing the "right" thing. This is the beginning of authenticity, that sacred rebellion inviting us to stop performing and start truly living. It isn't easy. No one warns you that being yourself can trigger rejection, discomfort, or even passive-aggressive family memes. But the relief of no longer lying to yourself far outweighs the fear of judgment.

Being authentic does not mean telling everything or showing off on social networks as if transparency were synonymous with exposure. It's all about consistency. To speak, dress, love, work, and dream from a place that makes no apologies for existing. And yes, sometimes that place is weird, misunderstood, or downright uncomfortable for others. But for yourself, it's home. A home without traps or cardboard, where one no longer needs masks, or permission.

The process is not linear. There are days when authenticity feels like a flag in the wind, and others when it looks like a "wanted" sign at the emotional police station. There will be those who applaud your new version, and those who want to return you to the old pigeonhole with a hypocritical smile and a phrase like "I preferred you as you were before". But that phrase, far from hurting, becomes proof that you are on the right track. Because no one bothers those who do not move.

The echo of silence and the call to authenticity are not enemies. They are partners in the beautiful crime of meeting you. One sets the alarm and the other shows you the way. And yes, maybe it hurts, but it hurts like when you take off your shoes at the end of the day: you realize how much they were squeezing you. And believe me, walking barefoot, even if it soils your feet, cleanses your soul.

The Weight of Invisibility: Exploring the experience of living with a hidden part of oneself.

Living with a hidden part of yourself is like carrying an invisible backpack full of emotional bricks. From the outside no one sees it, so no one offers help, but inside one walks every day with one's body bent and one's soul on tiptoe. The most ironic thing is that, by hiding who you are, you often achieve exactly what you fear: isolation, misunderstanding, distance. Invisibility does not protect, even if it promises to; what it does is slowly erase the traces that one could leave in the world. And of course, when you disappear a little bit every day, there comes a time when you don't even remember where you left off.

From psychology, this phenomenon has many labels: dissociation, repression, defense mechanisms. But in everyday life it manifests itself in automatic smiles, vague responses, changes of subject and an almost artistic ability to dodge uncomfortable conversations. It is not about cowardice. It's emotional survival. Because showing yourself as you can cost you affection, work, respect... or so you think. And that belief is domestic. Thus, one becomes one's own editor, crossing out words, gestures, tastes, and desires from one's personal history so as not to break the social script.

The problem is that the body doesn't lie. You can fake it all you want, but your nervous system knows something is wrong. The tension in the shoulders, the insomnia for no reason, the chronic sadness that appears right after happy moments, all that is the price of maintaining the façade. Because being invisible is different from being free. The first thing is strategy. Second, a conquest.

And yet, the world applauds you for how well you do. For not making you uncomfortable, for adapting, for "taking the party in peace". What they don't tell you is that while you try to make sure that no one notices that hidden part, others do the same with theirs. We all live surrounded by ghosts disguised as functional people, applauding normality as if it were an achievement and not a shared prison.

Sometimes invisibility begins in childhood, when we are taught that certain feelings are inappropriate, certain ideas are dangerous, or certain identities are "touchy." Then one learns to mask the difference as a sympathetic oddity, to soften the edges so as not to scratch. But over time, that mask no longer feels like an option: it becomes part of the skin. And removing it hurts, like peeling off a band-aid that has been attached to one's identity for years.

The good news is that visibility doesn't require megaphones or banners. Sometimes a sincere gesture, a phrase said without filters, a yes or no that they do not apologize is enough. Becoming visible is a process, not a one-time heroic act. And while it feels like walking around naked in a room full of judges at first, you eventually discover that many of those judges are just as scared, hiding under their emotional robes.

Invisibility weighs heavily. But authenticity, even if it costs, liberates. And as scary as it may be, showing yourself to the world as you are less exhausted than keeping the lie alive. Because deep down, we all want to be seen. Not admired, not approved, just seen. And that, although it may not seem like much, is the most revolutionary thing a human being can do.

The Promise of Authenticity: Why Is Being Yourself So Liberating, and Scary?

Authenticity promises something that, in theory, sounds irresistible: to live without masks, without filters, without having to remember which version of oneself was used with each person. Being yourself seems like a kind of emotional paradise where you breathe deeply, fall asleep without knots in your stomach and answer without calculating every word. It is fertile ground for inner peace, the kind of life where you no longer need to rehearse in front of the mirror what you are going to say, because what you have to say no longer needs emotional translation. However, just when one approaches that desired state, fear appears, like those annoying ads that interrupt just when the video gets good.

And being yourself has a price. It doesn't cost money, but it does cost ties, customs, places, and even emotional surnames. Because the world isn't always ready to deal with an unwrapped version of you. Deep down, many relationships survive thanks to the unsaid, the hidden, the edited. Showing yourself as you are puts all that in danger. And the idea of losing acceptance, belonging, or love for simply being is such a potent threat that most prefer to continue playing a role. From psychology, this is called fear of social rejection, but in practice it translates as "I'd better shut up", "it's not the time" or "why ruin it".

The most curious thing is that many times we are not afraid that people will see the worst of us, but the truest of us. Because the real thing makes us vulnerable. He has no excuses, no strategies, no alibis. There is no way to protect yourself when you show something genuine. It's like going out without an umbrella knowing that the sky threatens a storm. But also, when you finally do it, you feel almost childlike relief. Like taking off your shoes after an awkward party. Like coming home after pretending you love the city. That's when you understand that freedom is not doing what you want but about stopping asking permission to exist.

The scary thing about authenticity is that it is irreversible. Once you know what it feels like to be yourself, there's no going back. The feign becomes unbearable. Forced environments are more noticeable. Diplomatic phrases scratch. And yes, you are left with fewer people around, but closer to you. That is the true promise: no longer having to choose between being loved or being real. Because when one holds firmly from what it is, the love that comes no longer requires disguises. And that, although it is not numerous, is profoundly sufficient.

Authenticity, then, is not a goal but a daily practice. It is not reached once and kept as a trophy, but is constantly chosen, even when the voice or the heart trembles. Even when you know you might lose something. But every time you do it, even if it's with fear, you get a little piece of yourself back. And that is more valuable than any applause borrowed. In the end, being yourself doesn't guarantee instant happiness, but it does guarantee that no matter what, you won't have to betray yourself to survive. And that, in a world full of masks, is already a form of revolution.

Anxiety: The Alarm That Never Goes Off

Living with a façade is like having a burglar alarm activated 24/7, but inside your chest. Anxiety does not ask, does not warn, does not respect schedules; It sneaks into the throat during meetings, dates, or even while shopping for bread. From the psychological point of view, this constant tension derives from the internal vigilance that one exercises over oneself so as not to reveal "too much". The brain goes into hyperalert mode: Am I saying the right thing? Am I acting as expected? Did you notice that my eyelids are shaking? The sympathetic nervous system lives with its foot on the accelerator and the body, which is not stupid, ends up exhausted. The irony is that the attempt to fit in ends up leaving the real self out of focus. And all to look "normal", as if that existed outside of a washing machine.

Depression: The False Smile Tires

When you spend too much time pretending, sadness doesn't go away: it disguises itself. Depression, in this context, usually leads to a wardrobe of success, efficiency and social courtesy. You smile in the photos, you answer "all right" reflexively, but inside it's like living in a house without windows. From psychology, this phenomenon is known as emotional dissonance: the abyss between what is felt and what is shown. The result is a progressive wear and tear on the spirit, a kind of invisible mourning for oneself. You lose the taste of life while chewing on the routine with the face of a toothpaste commercial. And the worst thing: no one notices because you have become an expert in the performance of your life.

Cognitive Dissonance: The Brain Divided into Two Sides

Few things wear you down as much as betraying yourself in slow motion. And no, it doesn't have to be something big. Just say yes when you wanted to shout no, laugh at a joke that made you uncomfortable, or applaud an idea you actually loathe. These small acts, repeated day after day, set up an emotional bomb that not even the most expensive mindfulness can deactivate. It's called cognitive dissonance, but we could also call it "the internal cold war" where you are the two parties in conflict.

The human mind, while brilliant, is quite dramatic when you give it two opposing commands. If you believe in freedom, but you dress up with the opinion of others; if you value honesty but feign enthusiasm for things that don't move you a hair... Sooner or later, something cracks inside you And that's when that feeling of "something is not right, and I don't know what it is" appears. Surprise: it's you, living in a contradictory way.

This short circuit does not warn with red lights. It manifests itself in inexplicable tiredness, in anxiety that does not understand reasons, in an existential insomnia that does not improve with valerian tea or yoga at six in the morning. Because it is not work stress. It's emotional exhaustion from holding a version of yourself that is nothing like what you value.

And the worst thing is that the mind not only gets confused, but it also gets angry. When your actions do not coincide with your beliefs, the brain begins to look for absurd excuses to justify the disorder: "if I say what I think, I will lose friends", "I better keep quiet and not make a mess", "there will be time to be me". But time doesn't wait for you. And every time you procrastinate on your authenticity, something inside you learns that pretending is safer than being.

So, if you feel like you're moving forward, but you get tired as if you're running uphill all day, check to see if you're living coherently. Because living with the handbrake on doesn't just damage the car... it also ruins the trip. And you didn't come into this life to jerk around. You come to drive with the windows open, with music you like, and with the peace of knowing that, although the road is not always easy, at least you are walking it, being you. No masks. No mental civil war. And no desire to move to a cabin in the Himalayas. Although, if you still leave... that is because you felt like it. Not because your truth no longer has a place in your own life.

Emotional Exhaustion: Tired of Being Other

There is a type of exhaustion that is not noticeable to the naked eye, but it is felt even in the bones. It is that tiredness that does not come from the body, but from the soul. It is not cured by sleeping more hours, or turning off the phone, or going out on a weekend to "clear your head". It's silent wear and tears that builds up when, day after day, you pretend to be someone you're not. When inside you break, but on the outside you smile. When you no longer know if you are fulfilling a routine or playing a role that you did not even ask to play.

Maintaining a façade is like carrying an emotional backpack around the clock. But not just any backpack: one that changes shape depending on who's looking at you. Is it time to be the kind one who never gets angry? The quiet one that doesn't cause problems. The strong who can do everything and never shows weakness? Each version demands emotional memory, control, and constant effort. And that, although many see it as adaptation or education, ends up draining you inside. It's not that you can't take it anymore... you don't know how to continue without getting lost in the attempt.

This kind of exhaustion doesn't make a sound. He does not scream. It does not warn. It simply settles in like an internal fog that extinguishes your desire, your creativity, your presence. You keep delivering, you keep producing, you keep working. But something in you is fading, slowly, without making a fuss. And when you finally have some free time, you don't know whether to rest or cry. Because what hurts is not what you did, but everything you had to hide to do it.

From emotional psychology, this phenomenon is known as identity burnout: that state of mental and emotional fatigue that arises not from what you do, but from what you pretend while doing it. You're present, but you're not being you. You're smiling, but inside you're wondering if someone, one day, will be able to see the unfiltered version. The one that doesn't adapt, the one that doesn't edit every word, the one that doesn't apologize for making people uncomfortable.

And yes, many times we pretend out of love, out of fear, out of habit. To avoid conflicts. For protecting others from what we really feel. But in the long run, protecting the world so much from your truth ends up making you invisible even to yourself. How can you not be tired if you have been acting for years so that no one rejects you?

The hardest thing is that this tiredness is not always noticeable on the face. Sometimes it is noticeable in the tense body, in insomnia, in apathy, in the lack of motivation, in that feeling of being on autopilot. And when someone tells you "take a day off", you think: yes, but... free from whom? From others or from this version of me that I invented to survive.

Because sometimes what you need most is not a break from work, but a break from pretending. A breath without scripts. A space where you can say what you really feel without fear that it will ruin everything. A time where you don't have to worry about being misunderstood, judged, or corrected. Just you, no frills, no fear, no mask.

And that kind of rest, even if it doesn't come in the form of a vacation, can be life changing. Because when you finally give yourself permission to let your guard down, even for an instant, you begin to recover something you thought you had lost: your vital energy, your own voice, your true desire to be there.

So don't feel weak from getting tired. Getting tired of pretending is also valid. And giving yourself permission to be you, even if it's not perfect, even if not everyone likes it, is the first step to healing that deep tiredness that no one else can see... but you do. And it's time to listen to it.

The fear of rejection: when the "What if they don't like me?" It becomes a mantra.

Few things are as democratic as the fear of rejection. From those who avoid speaking in public to those who do not send a message so as not to appear "intense", we have all felt that uncomfortable knot that appears when the possibility of being judged enters the scene. Psychologically, this fear has deep roots: we have been programmed since caveman times to depend on the group. Being expelled from the clan meant dying of cold, hunger or boredom. Today we are not chased by wolves, but social networks can be just as cruel.

The Primary Wound: Not Being Enough

Behind the fear of rejection there is usually an unresolved childish belief: "If I show who I am, they will not love me". This idea, although irrational, is installed early and is fed by comments, looks, comparisons and traumas that we accumulate like emotional stamps. From the psychology of attachment, if as children we associate love with conditions (behave well, don't cry, be strong), as adults we learn to edit parts of ourselves for fear of losing affection. The result: we turn our relationships into permanent auditions.

Cognitive distortion: "Everyone is watching me."

The mind is adept at inflating realities. Someone else's laughter, an awkward silence, or an unanswered "seen" can become irrefutable evidence that "you didn't like you." This phenomenon has a name: catastrophic thinking. It's about imagining the worst-case scenario and acting like it's already happening. It's like having an internal radio that repeats "you're going to look like a fool" on a loop. And in the meantime, the other person is probably just thinking about what to have for dinner.

The Divided Self: Being Accepted or Being Authentic

Here the great dilemma arises: do I want to please or do I want to be me? When the fear of rejection dominates, many people choose to mold themselves according to what they believe the other wants. But this strategy comes at a cost: the real self begins to feel invisible, as a secondary actor in his own life. In the long term, the accumulation of micro-resignations generates frustration, loss of identity and the feeling of not belonging anywhere, not even to oneself. A cruel irony, because in an attempt to avoid being rejected, one ends up rejecting oneself.

What if I am rejected? Well, let them do it in style.

Accepting that not everyone likes you is liberating and, in a way, quite funny. Because you spend years trying to please, as if it were a human resume that must be approved by every person you come across. You smile when you don't want to, you turn down the volume on your personality, you edit your opinions as if they were a controversial tweet... and all for what. Spoiler: there may be people who misunderstand you, block you, avoid you or simply look at you as if you were a puzzle without instructions.

And therein lies the catch: we believe that if we try hard enough, we will be that universally acceptable person. But that does not exist. Not everyone likes chocolate, and you're not a Swiss bar. Rejection is inevitable. The key is not to avoid it, but to learn to look at it head-on without it taking you out of the game. Because many times that "I don't like the way you are" comes more from what the other person can't accept in themselves than from something really bad in you.

Learning to deal with it is like learning to dance. At first, it's clumsy: you justify yourself; you feel guilty, you wonder if you did something wrong. But then, when you realize that people judge you even when you're well-behaved, something in your head clicks. And that click sounds something like this: "What if instead of spending energy on pleasing, I invest it in being happy?"

And no, fear does not disappear. It's not that you suddenly become emotional steel. Only fear no longer has the microphone. It becomes a murmur in the background, not the director of the play. He no longer rules. You hear it, you understand it, but you don't give it the keys to the car.

When you accept that your value does not depend on the opinions of others, you begin to live lighter. You find that it's more important to respect yourself than to convince someone that you're "cool." And that day, even if there is no applause or fireworks, you begin to feel something new and powerful: freedom. A freedom that does not come from everyone who likes it, but from not needing it. And that, my friend, is one of the greatest signs of maturity... and also, why not, self-love with a sense of humor.

The Invisible Prisons: When the Cell Is Made of "Should"

You don't need to be behind bars to feel trapped. It is enough to grow up in a family that says, "that's not for you", live in a society that imposes what success should look like, or hear that one must swallow what one feels "so as not to look bad". The invisible prisons are not seen, but they feel like a weight on the chest. From psychology, this is called normative conformity: the impulse to belong often leads us to juggle emotionally in order to fit in. And the worst thing is that sometimes we don't even know why we follow that script... only that getting out of it is scary.

The mold is already made you just get comfortable.

From childhood we are taught, directly or indirectly, how we should be. Some commands are loud "When will the children be?" — and others insinuate themselves with silences, glances or comments disguised as advice. This is how a kind of mental list is formed: have a partner, study something "serious", do not talk too much about what is uncomfortable, avoid the strange. Little by little, one moves away from what one really wants to live according to what others expect. The problem is that afterwards we don't know if we are happy or simply good actors.

The family: the first emotional school

Family is our first mirror. There we learn what is worth feeling, who can be questioned, how to get approval and what parts of us should be hidden. Many times they do not do it out of malice, but because they repeat what they were also taught. But those mandates are staying inside, as if we were bringing an internal judge with a megaphone. Phrases such as "don't be ashamed", "no one will love you like this" or "men don't cry" dig into the unconscious and then repeat themselves, even when no one says them anymore.

Pride of others does not fill one's own emptiness.

Many live looking for their mother to feel proud, for their friends not to criticize them or for no one to "leave them in sight" for being different. That need for external approval becomes a broken compass: it moves you forward, but not where you want to go. Even if you get what everyone expected of you, sometimes you feel like something is missing. Because if you need others to validate every step you take, your life is no longer yours, but a showcase decorated with prizes that you don't know if you won or were loaned.

Being oneself: a radical act

Deciding to be authentic, in a world that teaches you to pretend, is a form of rebellion. Of course it makes you uncomfortable, of course it scares... but it also liberates. From humanistic psychology, being without masks is the path to self-realization. And yes, perhaps there are those who do not understand it, those who distance themselves or speak badly.

But living pretending to make others comfortable is an emotional prison without windows. On the other hand, when you dare to be you, even with doubts and stumbles, you discover that freedom is not doing what you want but stopping betraying yourself.

And if one day you feel like you don't fit in, maybe it's because you were born for something bigger than a mold. Perhaps, instead of asking permission to be you, it's time to build a place where you don't have to apologize for existing as you are.

The culture of "should be": manuals that no one asked for, but we all follow.

From the moment we are born, we are given an invisible script. "This is what is expected of you." And without realizing it, we begin to act according to that script: to be obedient, productive, pleasant, successful, thin, smiling, available, discreet. The culture of "should be" is that voice that does not shut up and repeats "you should be doing something useful", even when you are trying to rest. From psychology, this is related to the formation of the superego: that part of the mind that absorbs social and family norms until they become internal rules. The problem is that it doesn't distinguish between what you want and what others imposed, it just screams at you that you're not enough if you don't comply with everything.

Fitting in as an extreme sport

Living under the pressure of fitting in is like trying to fit into jeans two sizes smaller: uncomfortable, frustrating, and suffocating. This need to belong pushes us to hide emotions, aspirations, tastes and even opinions so as not to "get out of the mold". In psychological terms, it is a form of self-censorship that, over time, generates an internal disconnection. You start talking as expected, dressing according to the occasion, saying "yes" even if it burns your tongue. And at the end of the day, you don't know if they love you for who you are or how well you pretend.

The trap of other people's success

The culture of "should be" also comes with its own ranking: the one who works more is worth more, the one who marries young won, the one who does not have children was left behind. Everything is measured, everything is compared, as if life were a competition of achievements that no one asked to run. And there we are, tired and anxious, trying to reach a goal that changes every time we think we are close. The cruelest thing is that many times, when you achieve what was supposed to make you happy, you discover that it was not your dream, but someone else's.

The Price of Not Meeting the Mold

Those who dare to disobey the script sometimes pay dearly: they are judged, isolated, criticized, or turned into the subject of family gossip. The culture of "ought to be" punishes difference and rewards obedience, even if that obedience suffocates you. From a psychological point of view, this dynamic generates what is known as existential dissonance: a deep discomfort between what you feel and what you experience. And that discomfort does not disappear with motivational phrases... it creeps in, accumulates and explodes in the form of anxiety, insomnia or that famous "I don't know what's wrong with me".

Breaking the mold without breaking yourself

Getting out of that circle is not easy, but it is necessary. It involves reviewing your beliefs, distinguishing which ones are yours and which ones you inherited without question, and starting to build a life that represents you, not crushes you. Humanistic psychology proposes reconnecting with your authenticity as an act of healing. Because at the end of the day, we didn't come into the world to be well-edited copies, but unique versions — even if sometimes we're weird, intense, chaotic, or stubborn. So, if you're going to break something, let it be the mold, not your essence.

And remember: if we were all what we "should be," the world would be a giant office full of forced smiles and bored souls. Better to be you, with all the emotional spelling mistakes.

Consequences In Relationships: When The Costume Falls In Love First

Living with a mask has an inevitable consequence: whoever approaches you is not getting to know the real person, but the character you created to please. And of course, at first it works. You seem charming, successful, always in a good mood, never too intense. But holding that idealized version is exhausting, and when you start to show yourself as you are, the other person feels that they changed the channel without warning. From psychology, this is called lack of congruence between the real self and the social self, and it generates fragile bonds, where the fear of abandonment grows along with frustration.

Loving from insecurity: the recipe for self-sabotage

If you believe that you don't deserve to be liked for who you really are, you will unconsciously seek out relationships where you have to constantly prove your worth. Then you give more than you can, you keep quiet about what hurts you, you adapt to everything, you ask for little, and you stay, even if something is not right... as long as it is not rejected. In psychology this is understood as a form of insecure attachment: the more afraid you are of losing the other, the more you move away from yourself. And so a couple of three is formed: you, the other person, and the character you created to feel worthy of love.

Superficial connection: everything seems good, but nothing feels deep.

When it's not you, you also can't know if the link is true. Do they want you or your edited version? Do they listen to you, or do they only applaud what fits? This constant doubt prevents us from relaxing, trusting, and opening up emotionally. Relationships become like elevator chat: pleasant, but without substance. In therapy, many people describe this as a feeling of emotional emptiness despite being accompanied. Because when you hide what you really think, need or fear, you condemn yourself to a bond where intimacy is impossible.

The boomerang effect: when faking ends up pushing away.

Paradoxically, what one does to be accepted usually causes the opposite effect. By not showing yourself authentic, the relationship does not withstand conflicts, differences, or moments of vulnerability. And if by some miracle it is sustained, it does not satisfy. Because there is a part of you that knows that it is alone, even in company. From the systemic approach, relationships that are built from fear end up reproducing that same fear. You isolate yourself more trying to please, and you end up feeling rejected without anyone having rejected you yet.

The freedom to be you: even if your voice trembles, even if everyone doesn't applaud.

Loving beautiful is not loving perfect. It is to love from what you are, with what you have, and sometimes, even with what you lack. Authentic connections require courage, not emotional makeup. They require you to stand in front of the other without shields, without rehearsed speeches, with your laughter at the wrong time, your strange silences, your half-closed wounds and that delicious clumsiness of someone who wants well but doesn't always know how.

Showing yourself as you are scared because it means losing. Losing people, losing approval, losing control of the image. But what remains after that filter of sincerity is worth gold: people who not only put up with you but choose you. That they don't get scared if one day you're broken, that they don't leave when you tell them "I don't know", and that they stay even when the script falls apart.

Humanistic psychology said it elegantly, but we will say it more quickly: you do not make anyone fall in love with your mask of emotional stability or with your pristine affective curriculum. You fall in love with your unpolished version. With your bad jokes, your laugh that looks like a car alarm, your anger when you get hungry and that strange mixture between tenderness and chaos that you are when you feel safe.

And of course, showing that can cause some to flee. But what did you gain by keeping them close if what they loved was a character? Why do you want to fill your life with people who only applaud your edited part, if what hurts, heals, dreams, and loves in you is behind the scenes?

Because if you're not really present in your relationships, then who's there? A recycled version of you to please? A romantic comedy scripted you. A socially acceptable copy?

The relationships that heal, that nourish, that make you grow, are not the ones that look good in photos. They are the ones that hurt sometimes, but they do not betray. Those that are built with uncomfortable sincerity, not with emotional diplomacy. And that requires a daily decision: to be there. Really. With everything you are. Without hiding the laughter, without polishing the tears, without changing the dream.

Because in the end, true love doesn't need you to be perfect. It just needs to be you. And that, even if it sometimes feels like too little... that's all.

The Inner Scream: Recognizing Who You Are

There is a moment in life when you can no longer act. It doesn't matter how polished the costume is or how much applause you get for the character you play. Suddenly, something inside you shakes, rolls, plants. That something does not ask for permission or express itself elegantly. It is an inner cry, sometimes silent but deafening, which says: "I can no longer pretend." From existential psychology, this type of internal rupture usually arises in moments of crisis: a loss, a betrayal, a deep loneliness, or simply the fatigue of living a life that does not represent you. It is then that the soul – or the unconscious if you prefer the technical term – decides to stop cooperating with the deception.

The epiphany: more annoying than divine

Although movies sell us the epiphany as a scene with epic music and redemptive tears, in real life it is usually more like an anxiety attack with sweating and the desire to run aimlessly. Acknowledging who you are doesn't always feel pretty; Sometimes it feels like finding out that you've been lying to yourself for years without meaning to. It's looking back and thinking, "And I did all of this just to fit in?" From therapy, many describe this moment as waking up in someone else's house, where everything is settled, but nothing feels their own. The discomfort does not go away... until you decide to stop accommodating yourself.

The Undeniable: When You Can't Close Your Eyes Anymore

There is a moment when you can no longer be distracted. That inner truth that I barely murmured before, begins to scream at you from within. And it doesn't matter how many series you watch, how many excuses you build or how much you hide behind "it's not that bad"... because you already know it. You know who you are, what breaks you, what you yearn for, and what you are not willing to continue tolerating. And once you know, faking it becomes suffocating.

That is the point of no return. Not because the world ends, but because another one opens up. One that no longer accepts that you live as a copy, as a mold, as someone else's expectation. From the psychology of the self, that moment is individuation: the deep self-coming out of the basement, kicking doors, demanding oxygen. It is no longer enough to comply. Now it is necessary to be. To be you. Even if everything trembles.

And yes, it's scary. Because for a long time that armor you were wearing seemed to protect you. It made you fit in. It gave you the role of the ideal child, the perfect partner, the harmless friend. But there comes a day when that armor does not warm, it only weighs. And continuing to use it is no longer courage, it is self-abandonment. Because when something inside you starts hurting from holding a lie, you're no longer choosing peace: you're avoiding conflict... at your expense.

What is liberating is not external change. It's not coming out, quitting a job, breaking up a relationship, or moving to a new country — although sometimes it comes with that, too. What it releases is internal permission. That sacred instant when you honestly say to yourself: no more. I don't want to live half-heartedly anymore. I no longer want my silence to cost me my joy. I no longer want to continue disguising pain as diplomacy.

And of course, not everyone is going to applaud this transformation. Some will walk away, others will question, and there will be those who will try to return you to your old version because it is more comfortable for them. But you will know that there is no going back. Because, even if you don't know what the new path is like yet, the old one no longer feels like home.

Taking off your armor is the greatest act of rest you can give yourself. Not because the world suddenly becomes soft, but because you can finally breathe without filters, move without guilt, and look in the mirror without dodging your gaze.

That's you. As is. No disguise. No script. And although fear is still there, the important thing is that now you walk with it... but in the end you are going in your direction.

Now what? When the cry calls for action

Revelation is not enough. It is followed by an uncomfortable question: "What are you going to do with this truth?" Changing courses, speaking clearly, asking for help, saying "no", breaking ties, starting therapy, changing careers, coming out of the emotional closet... whatever. But something has to move. The inner scream is not only an alarm signal, but also a compass. Ignoring it can make the body sick, poison relationships, or shut down vitality. Listening to him, on the other hand, begins the path towards a more coherent life. Not perfect, not easy, but more yours.

The truth doesn't always go down well, but it relieves.

Recognizing who you are does not come with a reward, but it does come with loss. Sometimes it means that certain friends drift away because you no longer serve as a polished mirror for them. Or that the family is disappointed because you are no longer the ideal project they built in their head. Your partner may even look at you as if you changed the language without warning. But showing yourself is not treason. It's rescue. Because if in the process of pleasing everyone you lost yourself, then who were they loving?

The famous "inner scream" doesn't always sound like an opera. Sometimes it's just a whisper, a dull annoyance, a discomfort that tells you "this is not who you are". He does not come to ruin your life, but to give it back to you. It tells you that there's a huge difference between surviving by doing what's right for others and actually living from who you are, even if it's uncomfortable.

Because when you silence that voice for too long, the void is not filled with likes, or with a partner, or with diplomas. Everything feels hollow. You can have it all and feel like you have nothing, simply because you're not inhabiting yourself. You are a functional shell. A professional of the acceptable. An expert in looking good. But what about you?

When you finally listen to yourself and decide to respond, something changes. It's not like the world suddenly understands you. It's that you stop asking permission. You stop apologizing for feeling different, loving differently, dreaming differently. And you start building from within, without someone else's manual. With doubts, with mistakes, with tears... but with dignity.

Yes, the cost may be high. But living on autopilot, adapting to other people's molds, costs you much more: it costs you peace. It costs you true laughter.

You have a hard time feeling that you are in your life, and not in someone else's.

So, if today you feel that something inside you wants to talk, don't silence it. Don't put music on it. Listen to me. Even if it bothers you. Because that voice, for the first time, is not asking for attention: it is asking for freedom. And you, more than anyone else, deserve it.

Challenging the "should": breaking with imposed narratives.

The "should" are like small social alarms that settle in the head from an early age: "you should behave well", "you should lose weight", "you should be married now", "you should have children", "you should be more grateful, more positive, stronger, quieter, more everything". They are phrases that sound like advice, but in reality, they are disguised orders. From cognitive psychology, these "should" be distortions of thought that generate guilt, frustration and a constant pressure to reach standards that were almost never consciously chosen. Breaking with these narratives is not an act of childish rebellion, it is a vital step towards emotional autonomy.

The invisible weight of the "ought to be."

Living according to what you "should" do is like walking with a backpack full of rocks that others put on you while you only asked for directions. The problem is that we often carry that backpack with pride, believing that being "good" is the same as being obedient. In psychological consultation, it is common to hear people who have everything "in order", but do not know why they feel empty. And it is that following a borrowed life, even if it is socially approved, ends up wearing out the soul. Living is different from playing the role well.

The fault: the security guard of the "should"

Every time one goes off script, guilt appears as if it were an emotional supervisor with a badge. "Are you really going to leave that stable job for something you are passionate about?", "And what is your mom going to think?", "What if you regret it?" Guilt does not come alone; it brings shame, fear, and existential doubts. But the curious thing is that many times we are not breaking a natural law but disobeying an alien expectation that does not even represent us. From systemic psychology, challenging these narratives is also an act of generational healing: not only do you free yourself, but you stop inheriting chains.

The risk of being you: more real, less comfortable.

Questioning the "should" is not for the faint-hearted. It involves dismantling internal structures, disappointing loved ones, and sometimes running out of certainties for a while. But that momentary void is necessary to build from scratch. Humanistic psychology holds that authenticity is not achieved by filling in boxes, but by questioning the boxes themselves. Maybe you shouldn't "should" anything. Maybe you just can. You can choose, change your mind, explore what is good for you without apologizing for not meeting the mold.

And if you're going to break something... Let it be the narrative, not your desire.

Every time you dare to say "this is not for me" while everyone applauds otherwise, you are signing a declaration of emotional independence. Not with fireworks, but with the firmness of someone who begins to live without the permission of others. That phrase, as small as it may seem, is a barricade against what should be, against what people will say, against the "way it is done". And even if your voice trembles, even if you feel that you betray expectations, what you are really doing... is coming back to you.

Choosing differently is not arrogance. It's self-care. It's having tasted the mold and realizing that it squeezes your soul. And of course, there will always be those who get upset when you stop playing the role that suited them. Because many are not bothered by what you do, but that you do it from your truth and not from theirs.

But magic is in what starts to come when you leave space. People who approach not because of the mask, but because of the essence. Links that don't require you to edit. Conversations where you don't have to be translated. Relationships that do not seek to please you, but to embrace you.

To break with the "should" is to stop being accountable to a list of expectations that no one signed with you. It's looking in the mirror and not only recognizing yourself but respecting yourself. And that, in a world where we teach to please rather than to be, is a profoundly rebellious act.

Because pretending is easy. The difficult thing is to be yourself when no one guarantees you applause. But there's the catch: you don't need standing ovations when you finally stop betraying yourself. The relief of living without duplicity, without performances, without borrowed smiles, is priceless.

So whenever you choose your peace over your popularity, remember this: you're doing more than deciding. You are showing freedom. You're giving your story a voice of its own. And in a society that values appearance more than consistency, that's not just an act of courage... It is a silent revolution with an eternal echo.

Breaking the Silence: First Steps Outward

Coming out of the emotional hiding place doesn't always start with a great speech or a dramatic revelation. Sometimes it starts with something as simple as saying "I don't want to go" without making excuses, wearing the clothes you like, even if no one else likes it, or daring to say "it hurts" when you always pretend everything was fine. Those small gestures, those micro revelations, are more powerful than they seem. From the psychology of personal development, each of these acts builds a bridge between the real self and the self that shows itself to the world. And although the first step seems insignificant, it is the one that breaks the pattern of silence that you have been repeating for years.

The first "no" that didn't know guilt.

Saying "no" when you're used to pleasing is like letting go of a dragon you had locked up. At first it is scary. You are afraid of hurting, disappointing, losing affection. But when you do it and discover that the world is not falling apart, something changes. You realize that setting boundaries doesn't make you selfish, but human. In therapeutic terms, that first "no" marks the entrance to the strengthened self-concept: an image of yourself that is no longer based on how much you endure, but on how much you respect yourself.

Small truths that open doors

Sometimes, a single sentence said from honesty changes the tone of a relationship: "I'm not really comfortable with that," "I'm interested in something different," "I've been feeling weird lately." You don't need to confess your whole soul all at once; just let a little piece out and see what happens. These small openings generate a domino effect on personal confidence. Because every time you show yourself as you are and nothing terrible happens, your nervous system takes note: "I can survive this".

Thus, the old alarm of fear of rejection is deactivated.

Everyday Acts of Emotional Courage

Wearing the color you always avoid for fear of attracting attention, sharing an unpopular opinion, acknowledging that something hurt you, allowing yourself to cry in front of someone, saying "I'm tired of pretending"... All these actions are as small as they are revolutionary. They don't change the world, but they change yours. In psychology they are called behaviors of progressive emotional exposure. They are the way in which you slowly retrain your mind to accept the discomfort of being visible, without feeling that it amounts to being in danger.

When you start listening to yourself... Everything sounds different

Micro-revelations not only transform your relationships with others, but they also modify your relationship with yourself. You begin to listen to yourself more clearly, to detect when you are acting out of fear or desire, to distinguish your own voice from the inherited voice. And in that process, something appears that cannot be bought or faked: coherence. You are no longer in survival mode, but in presence mode. And although at first it hurts or discomforts, in the end it is lighter to live without so much contradiction.

Because opening your mouth to tell you the truth, even if it is little by little, is already an act of freedom. You may not notice it at first, but every little gesture counts. Every time you break the silence, even with a trembling voice, you are writing a new chapter. One where the protagonist is finally you.

Identifying Allies: Who Are Safe People In Your Life

On the road to authenticity, not everyone deserves a front-row seat. Some people come with scissors in their hands and others with thread and needles to help you patch them up. Knowing how to distinguish between one and the other is not only wise: it is vital. From the psychology of attachment and emotional intelligence, safe people are those with whom you can be yourself without fear of judgment, mockery, or abandonment. They don't need you to explain why you changed, they don't applaud you only when you act "right," and they don't disappear when your most vulnerable version rears its head.

The ones who stay when you don't pretend anymore.

An emotional ally is not the one who is alone in good times, but the one who is still there when you take off your costume. When you're not the nice, the strong, the successful one, the one who always has answers. Confident people don't need to look perfect to validate you. They don't condescend you or give you an emotional lecture every time you show yourself confused. They listen to you. They respect you. They allow you to exist as you are, even when they don't fully understand what you're experiencing. Because they know that real affection is not based on performance, but on presence.

Signs that you're with someone safe.

If you can share something difficult and you don't get “good, but at least...", if you can cry without being asked to dry your tears, if you can show your contradictions without being questioned about your worth, you are in front of an ally. Relational psychology talks about "emotional resonance": that phenomenon in which someone not only hears you but tunes in to you. These people don't minimize your emotions, label you as "dramatic," or use your confidence as ammunition in future discussions. Your company doesn't drain it relieves.

It's not quantity, it's quality (and mental health)

You don't need a support army. Sometimes it is enough for a single person to hold you with their eyes when you feel that you are disarmed. A friend, a therapist, a sibling, a partner, someone who is not afraid to see you change. Many times, identifying your true allies means accepting that they are not always who you expected. They may not be your blood family, but they are your chosen family. Because emotional security is not inherited, it is cultivated. And when you find it, the soul knows it: there you can rest.

And yes, there will be losses... but also encounters.

Breaking the mold is not only uncomfortable on the outside, but it also breaks on the inside. Because it hurts to realize that some relationships only existed to hold your mask, not your truth. And when that mask falls, there are silences that speak louder than any speech. People who stop calling, who move away awkwardly, who look at you as if you have broken the tacit contract of "continuing to act so as not to make you uncomfortable".

But among the rubble of what cools, something much warmer appears: the space for the authentic. When you stop pretending, you start to resonate with those who are also unwilling to continue representing. With people who don't need to see you perfectly want you present. That is not scandalized by your contradictions but celebrates them as part of the human package that we all are.

Your circle begins to change. And while it may feel like loneliness at first, what you're gaining is real intimacy. One of those that do not seek to decorate you, but to get to know you. It is no longer a question of quantity, but of emotional quality. Because a genuine link is worth a hundred acquaintances who are only comfortable with your edited version.

And that's where you discover something important: a good ally is not the one who comes to rescue you from pain, but the one who sits with you in it without running away. Who does not try to fix you, but to accompany you. Who is not frightened when your voice trembles, when you doubt, when you cry without a filter.

In a world full of relationships that shine but empty inside, finding someone to walk with you while you rebuild yourself, without judgment or haste, is an immense gift. Those are the links that don't go viral but save entire days.

So if you're at that point where everything seems to be shaky because you decide to be you... Hold. The discomfort is real, but it's also the first sign that you're building a life that doesn't fall to the first wind. And in that process, little by little, yours – the real ones – begin to arrive. They don't make a sound, but they stay. And in a world of easy applause, that's home.

Managing Fear and Vulnerability: Strategies for Coping with Initial Uncertainty

The first step towards authenticity is often accompanied by a healthy dose of fear. It's no coincidence: you're stepping out of your emotional comfort zone, dismantling years of automatism, breaking invisible contracts with your environment. From the psychology of change, this phase is called the dissonance phase, and it is characterized by an uncomfortable mixture of confusion, expectation, doubts, and the feeling of walking without a map. Vulnerability, in this context, is not weakness: it is a sign that you are doing something brave without guarantees. And yes, everything shakes, but that also means you're alive.

Normalize fear: it's not your enemy, it's your escort.

Fear is not the villain of this story; It's that clumsy bodyguard who tries to protect you even when there's no real danger anymore. He appears with his flashlight, looking for signs of rejection, criticism, or abandonment. But more often than not, those monsters he feared no longer existed or were never there. A helpful strategy is to learn to speak to that fear as if it were a nervous partner, not as an authority. "Thank you for taking care of me, but here I can move forward on my own." From cognitive-behavioral therapy, it is taught to reframe catastrophic thoughts, training the brain to see challenges instead of threats.

Small steps, big changes

You don't have to tell your soul to the world in one fell swoop. All it takes is a small but honest step: expressing an opinion that you used to keep quiet, showing an emotion that you used to hide, doing something that you always postponed for fear of "what people will say". Gradual exposure is an amazingly effective psychological technique: it is about facing fear in sections, like someone who enters a swimming pool by putting their feet in first.

Little by little, your mind adapts to that new emotional temperature, and what previously paralyzed you, begins to seem manageable.

Anchor in the real: routine, body and present

When mental uncertainty overwhelms, the body can be your refuge. Breathing deeply, moving, writing what you feel, drinking water, tidying up your space. These simple gestures don't solve the problem, but they help you not to sink into it. It's also key to establish small routines – something stable that you can hold on to while everything else is moving. From the approach of acceptance and commitment therapy (ACT), a lot of work is done with the idea of anchoring yourself in the present, making decisions aligned with your values, even if the emotion is uncomfortable.

Seek accompaniment: shared vulnerability is less burdensome.

You don't have to ride through the storm alone. Talking to someone you trust, sharing your doubts, seeking therapeutic support or groups that validate your experience can make all the difference. When you realize that you're not the only person dealing with fear of change, the load lightens. The simple act of being listened to without judgment has a regulatory effect on the nervous system. And when you dare to be vulnerable in front of another, you open the door to a deeper connection... and the kind of relief that is not bought is earned.

Celebrate courage, not the result.

Stepping out of the mold doesn't come with fireworks or epic music in the background. Many times, all you hear is the awkward silence of those who don't understand your change or the inner noise of your own fears kicking the door. But even without ovations, every authentic step is worthy of recognition. Not because of what you accomplished, but because of the simple, but immense, act of daring.

Because being you, with all that that implies—fears, doubts, scars, and the desire to run—is an act of everyday courage. One of those that don't appear on networks, but that change your life. And facing uncertainty without guarantees is a profound way of telling yourself: I trust myself, even if I don't yet fully know how.

Over time, it's not like the fear magically disappears. It's that you learn to sit in the back seat while you drive. You can give him water, even let him complain a little, but no more the steering wheel. Because fear is not the enemy, it is just the reminder that you are crossing an emotional boundary. And if you're scared, it's because it matters.

Real confidence is not born when everything is clear, but when you start walking even when everything is blurred. It is that soft and trembling certainty that tells you: I don't know what is coming, but I know that I have myself. And that is enough to continue.

And then there is vulnerability, that word that many confuse with weakness, when in reality it is the strongest muscle of the soul. Because showing yourself as you are, without armor or filter, does not make you fragile... it makes you human. Of flesh, blood and emotions that are not always explained, but are felt.

So, if today you woke up with a trembling voice and an exposed heart, but you still chose to be you... congratulations. You have just starred in a heroic act. Even if no one sees it. Even if there is no medal. Because living in coherence, even with fear, is already winning. And in a world full of pretty but empty molds, that makes you deeply real. And more real than that, impossible.

Negative responses: how to deal with rejection, misunderstanding, or hostility.

One of the biggest barriers to showing ourselves authentic is the possibility that someone will answer wrong. Sometimes, reality does not disappoint you open up and receive an awkward silence, a mockery, a criticism disguised as advice or directly a door in the face. From psychology, these responses activate areas of the brain related to physical pain – yes, it literally hurts – because rejection puts our sense of belonging at stake. But here's the important thing: just because something hurts doesn't mean it's dangerous. It means you're stepping out of the mold. And that, although it hurts, also strengthens you.

Not all rejection is personal (even if it seems like it)

When someone judges you for being you, they're really talking more about their own fears, beliefs, and boundaries than they are about you. There are people who react with discomfort because your authenticity reminds them of everything they have had to repress. In projective psychology, this is known as "mirror displeasure": they are bothered by what they do not dare to see in them. So the next time you thrown a "that's not right" or "you're getting weird," breathe. You're not failing, you're reflecting other's truths that not everyone is ready to look at.

Validate what you feel, without dramatizing everything.

Just because something affects you doesn't make you weak. It makes you aware. Accepting sadness, anger, or confusion in the face of a hostile response is part of the process. What doesn't help is sticking to rejection as if it defines your value. In emotional therapy, the art of feeling without amplifying is worked on a lot. Did it hurt? Yes. Is it worth thinking about it for weeks? Does it mean you have to hide again? Neither. Feeling is inevitable. Turning that into a judgment about yourself, it's not.

Filter the review: not every comment deserves a home in your head.

Not everything they tell you is valid, nor is everyone allowed to give an opinion about your life. When you receive criticism, ask yourself: is this coming from someone who knows me, who loves me well, who respects me? If it doesn't meet at least two of those conditions, mentally return it to the sender. In therapeutic practice, it is taught to distinguish between constructive feedback and simple emotional attacks. If they tell you with respect and affection, listen to it. If it comes with poison, don't take it... nor, even if it comes wrapped in beautiful words.

Protect your energy without becoming a wall.

It is not about closing yourself off from the world but about learning to shield yourself without hardening yourself. Setting limits is not building walls, it is placing filters. You can walk away without fighting, say "this doesn't work for me" without yelling, and keep your peace, even if someone doesn't understand your process. Emotional intelligence does not seek to avoid conflict, but to go through it with the least possible damage. And when you know that your authenticity is worth more than the acceptance of others, it hurts less to lose someone who did not know how to see it.

Rejection is not final, it is emotional natural selection.

There are answers that hurt, but that also awaken. When you show yourself as you are and someone reacts with contempt, judgment, or indifference, you are not losing space: you discover that it was never yours. The universe—life, your intuition, your soul, whatever you want to call is taking away from you what no longer sustains you. And yes, at first it burns. Rejection has edge, misunderstanding stings, and hostility can feel like an emotional slap. But if you look deeper, you'll understand that that jolt is a cleansing. A necessary pruning so that you do not continue to grow where you do not flower.

Because every "no" that comes when you express your truth is a mirror: it shows you what the other is not ready to see, what you are no longer willing to keep quiet, and what the bond does not have the capacity to sustain. And that's where the beautiful, if uncomfortable, part is revealed: not everyone is made to receive you completely. And that doesn't make you any less. It makes you more aware of who does.

Instead of spending yourself explaining why you feel what you feel, why you think what you think, why you love the way you love or fight for what you believe in, you can start directing that energy towards those who don't need you to cut back in order to hug you. Towards those who listen without interrupting, validate without conditioning, and accompany you without asking you to explain yourself every five minutes. Because if you have to reduce yourself to being accepted, that is not love... it is an emotional transaction.

The discomfort of others in the face of your authenticity is a great filter. Rejection is not punishment, it is direction. It's life pointing at you with brutal clarity: this is not your place, but you're already getting closer. Don't back down. Don't edit your essence only to re-enter a room where your soul no longer fits. Don't shut up what's real in you just to stay close to those who prefer you anesthetized.

Yes, it's going to hurt. They are going to leave you in sight. They are going to call you exaggerated, changing, complicated. But between you and the version you pretended to be, always choose to stay with you. Because at the end of the day, the only one who goes to bed with your conscience, with your thoughts, with your heart beating in the middle of your chest... it's you. And you deserve to rest in peace, not afraid that your truth will seem too much to someone else.

So whenever someone reacts badly to your truth, don't take it as a defeat. Take it for what it is: a purge. A natural rearrangement that is taking you, even if it hurts, towards bonds where you will no longer have to translate yourself. Where being you will not be a battle, but a relief. And where, at last, you will sleep peacefully... not because you fit in, but because you were honest. And that, believe me, is priceless.

Building Resilience: Strengthening The Inner Self In The Face Of Adversity

Resilience is not a superpower exclusive to the enlightened or a cheesy Instagram attitude. It is the very human – and quite sweaty – ability to recompose yourself after the blow, rejection or fall. From positive psychology, it is understood as the ability to adapt flexibly to difficult situations, without losing sight of who you are or letting pain erase your value. It's not about "being strong" all the time or pretending that nothing hurts you but about building an inner self capable of sustaining you even when everything else is faltering. Because being resilient is not being made of iron: it is being made of flesh, but with roots.

Accepting without giving up: the paradox that heals

One of the keys to building resilience is to accept that there are things you can't control... without becoming a passive victim of them. It sounds weird, but it works. Accepting is not giving up; it is stopping fighting with reality to start responding from your center. In therapy, this is called active acceptance: acknowledging the pain, looking the loss in the face, letting the sadness pass through you without settling in as a housewife. Because what you resist persists. But what you embrace is transformed.

The self-talk: Your inner voice can be your enemy or your lifeline.

When you're going through a crisis, how you talk to yourself is almost as important as the situation itself. "I'm a disaster", "this happens to me for a fool", "I'm never going to be able to"... These thoughts are not only cruel: they are useless. Resilience begins when your inner voice changes from judge to ally. Instead of crushing you, it accompanies you: "I'm going through something hard, but I'm not alone," "this doesn't define my value," "I can make mistakes and still keep growing." It's not magic, it's emotional neuroplasticity: training the brain to stop shooting darts at you when you're already on the ground.

Personal resources: you have more than you think.

Many people believe that they are not resilient until they have no other choice. And there appear tools that I didn't even know I had creativity to get out of the mess, a sense of humor so as not to explode, intuition to choose well, and, above all, emotional memory to remember that it is not the first time you get up. In psychotherapy, these internal strengths are explored as a kind of emotional medicine cabinet: everyone has their own, you just have to learn to open it. You don't need to have everything figured out. You need to know that you can improvise from what you do have.

Real support, not empty phrases

Part of resilience is also knowing how to ask for help. Not like "rescue me", but "walk with me for a while I rebuild". There is an abysmal difference between support that heals and that which only makes people uncomfortable ("everything happens for a reason", "be strong", "others are worse off"). Truly empathetic people do not bring solutions: they bring presence, respectful silence, and sometimes even a hot meal or a laugh at the wrong time. Being accompanied, without pressure or judgment, reminds your inner self that you are not alone on the battlefield.

Resilience is not about going back to the way you were before: it is building a new version from the wound.

It is often believed that being resilient is to return to how you were before the coup. But no. True resilience involves transformation. You are not the same after a loss, a betrayal, a breakup, or a failure. But that's not a bad thing. Resilience does not mend it reinvents. From narrative psychology, you can rewrite your story from pain, not to deny it, but to integrate it. And then, what was once a crack, becomes a root.

Because in the end, being resilient is not about preventing life from shaking you. It is learning to dance with shakes, although sometimes you lose the rhythm, but never the step.

Setting boundaries: protecting one's own energy and well-being

Setting limits is not being selfish, it is being aware that your well-being is not a luxury, but a basic need. Boundaries are like an emotional fence: not to push everyone away, but to protect what's inside. From relational psychology, establishing healthy boundaries involves recognizing your needs, your emotions, and your real capacity for surrender without feeling guilty for not being available 24/7. Because if you wear yourself out trying to please everyone, the only thing that's left of you... it is tiredness. And neither you nor anyone else can flourish from exhaustion.

When saying "yes" hurts you more than saying "no"

One of the clearest indicators that you need to set a limit is that knot in your stomach that appears every time you accept something you don't want. You do it out of commitment, out of fear of conflict, out of guilt... but then you feel uncomfortable, used, or invisible. In emotional psychology, this dissonance is worked on as a warning light: every time you automatically prioritize the other over you, you are negotiating your peace. And the worst part is that, in the long run, accumulating forced "yeses" turns into silent resentment. Saying "no" early saves you a lot of future therapies.

Boundaries are not walls: they are well-designed bridges.

The idea is not to isolate you or make you unapproachable. A good boundary doesn't say "walk away," it says "get closer this way." It's a way of teaching others how to treat you. From cognitive therapy, assertive communication is trained precisely for that: to express your limits without hurting, without shouting, without turning every situation into an emotional war. You can say "this doesn't do me any good", "I can't now", or "I'm not available for that" without sounding cold, but clear.

Because protecting yourself is not an act of violence: it is an act of self-love.

The fear of making people uncomfortable: the official saboteur of limits.

One of the great obstacles to setting limits is the fear of losing affection, of being seen as "difficult", or of causing disappointment. But here's an uncomfortable truth: if someone walks away because you set a limit for them, they were probably never there because of you, but because of what you gave them. Systemic psychology explains it as "bond restructuring": when you change your internal rules, some bonds are rearranged, and others are broken. It hurts; it hurts. But it also cleans. Because no one deserves your energy if they're just willing to take it, not respect it.

Reinforce your own limit: because sometimes you are the first to break it.

The problem is not only that others cross your boundaries, but that you yourself ignore them. You promise yourself not to respond to messages after a certain time... and you end up sending audios at one in the morning. You say you won't justify yourself again... And there you are, giving explanations as if you should be allowed to exist. Setting boundaries also means committing yourself. Not only saying "so far" to others but also reminding you when the old habit of pleasing wants to creep back in through the emotional window.

Your energy is yours: it is not rented, it is not given away, it is managed.

Many confuse boundaries with coldness, selfishness, or rejection. But the truth is that learning to say "that's it" doesn't mean you're building a wall, but you're drawing the map of your dignity. You're not pushing people away; you're marking from what point you can approach without ceasing to be you. In a world that wants you always available, always helpful, always in good spirits, even if inside you are falling apart, saying "I can't" or "I don't want to" is almost an act of spiritual disobedience. And that... it is respected.

Living on the defensive wears you down. But so does living without defenses. Balance is in knowing how to discern. Not everyone deserves unfettered access to you. Not everyone knows how to take care of what you share with them. Not everyone will interpret your surrender as an act of love and not as an obligation. Therefore, setting limits is not putting barriers, it is naming your energy, it is managing your emotional resources with awareness. Not because you lack love, but because you finally learned to love without sacrificing yourself.

People who really love you are not offended when you take care of yourself. On the contrary, he is grateful for it. Understand that an exhausted version of yourself is not the best you can offer, and that your presence is worth more when it comes from desire and not from obligation. On the other hand, those who get angry when you stop giving them everything, were probably never there for you, but for free access to your effort.

Setting limits is not about being blunt, dry, or distant. It's about being honest. To be able to look the other person in the eye and say: "I love you, but this is not good for me", or "I can be there, but not today", or simply "this is not for me". And whoever understands it, stays. And those who don't, leave. And if he leaves, it's because he wasn't prepared for the most honest version of you. And that, although it hurts, also liberates.

Because there is no deeper peace than that of being present without feeling used, without feeling that you disappear little by little so that others feel comfortable. When you protect your well-being, you say, "I recognize myself, I respect myself, I belong to myself." And from there, you can give without resentment, accompany yourself without annulling yourself, and love without having to erase yourself to be loved.

So don't be afraid of limits. They are the clearest way of saying "this is me, and I take care of myself enough not to give myself away to those who do not value me". Because those who learn to set limits do not become distant. It becomes real. And in a world where many live pretending to be accepted, being real is not only an act of self-love: it is a form of silent revolution that transforms everything it touches.

The importance of community: looking for spaces and people who accept you unconditionally.

No matter how strong you are, no one heals completely in solitude. Personal growth can be an inner journey, but validation, relief, and reflection of your truth are often found in the eyes of others. The community, from social psychology, is not only a support network: it is a network of recognition. Being with people who don't look at you funny for saying what you feel, who don't ask you for explanations for who you are, and who celebrate your existence without asking you to edit parts of yourself, is not a privilege: it's a basic emotional need. Because when you surround yourself with those who accept you unconditionally, you stop living on the defensive and start living to the fullest.

Being You Without Translation: The Relief Of Belonging Without Disguise

In safe spaces, you don't need to "tone it down", or soften your emotions, or triple-check your way of speaking so as not to make you uncomfortable. You can arrive with sadness on your back or overflowing laughter, and both states will be welcome. True community is that group where you don't have to explain your weirdness, because everyone has theirs. From group therapy to spontaneous community spaces, sharing the human experience with those who don't judge you generates a profound reparation: that of feeling that you are not alone, or crazy, or deviant... only human.

The mirror that heals seeing we in others, recognizing ourselves better

Sometimes you need someone else to tell you "it happened to me too" to realize that your story doesn't make you less. Listening, sharing, and resonating with others who have been through the same thing, or who simply don't want to change you, broadens your understanding of yourself. In humanistic psychology, this is called genuine encounter: a connection where both people see each other without filters, without demands, without masks. There, between the "me too" and the "I see you", a force is born that is not achieved in self-help books or in agenda phrases: it is called belonging.

Taking care of what takes care of you: the community is also watered.

It is not enough to find a safe space: it must also be nurtured. The community is a living exchange, not a la carte service. It involves showing yourself but also supporting others. Listen without interrupting. Support without invading. Celebrate the achievements of others without comparing yourself. Emotional reciprocity creates real bonds, and in those bonds, the self-expands. Because when others shine without overshadowing you, you understand that love is not scarce, conditional, or competitive. It is circular.

If you are not accepted, it is not community: it is an audience.

Sometimes we confuse community with a group of acquaintances, biological family, or old friends. But if those bonds require you to camouflage yourself, judge you when you speak honestly, or disappear when you go through a crisis, you're not in a community: you're acting on stage. And that is also exhausting. Looking for new spaces can be scary, especially if you grew up believing you were "too much" or "wrong." But I assure you that there are places out there where your voice doesn't just fit: it is needed. Finding them is an act of emotional justice.

Because when you're in a community that sustains you, nurtures you, and respects you, you flourish without realizing it. And not because you don't have wounds, but because at last there are those who look at them with you without rushing to close them. In this field, growth becomes more than possible: it becomes inevitable.

Solidarity and Mutual Support: How Connecting With Others In Similar Situations Strengthens

In the midst of the struggle to be yourself, discovering that you're not alone is like finding oxygen in a locked room. Solidarity is not just about comforting; it is about holding, reflecting, and walking alongside another who is going through the same storm with different shoes. From community psychology, mutual support generates what is known as shared empowerment: when you see someone survive what you are going through, your mind stops repeating "I can't" and starts whispering "me too". The connection between people with similar experiences isn't just comfort: it's emotional fuel.

The "Me Too" That Breaks Isolation

One of the deepest wounds of rejection or difference is isolation. Feeling weird, wrong, out of place... until someone else says "it happened to me too". That phrase, simple but powerful, has an immediate therapeutic effect: it disarms loneliness, lowers shame, takes you out of the inner cave. Trauma psychology speaks of the power of the compassionate witness: someone who does not give you advice, or solutions, or magic recipes... it just looks at you with real understanding and validates what you feel without judgment. Sometimes, that act is worth a thousand sessions.

When sharing does not weaken, but strengthens.

There is a harmful myth that says that talking about one's own wounds is victimizing oneself. But the reality is different: sharing from emotional honesty not only frees you but also gives others permission to do the same. Support groups, safe spaces, even deep friendships, allow pain to be transformed into a shared experience. From the humanistic approach, this is called reciprocal authenticity: when both people leave the ego at the door and show themselves as they are. Not to compete for who suffered the most, but to remind each other that moving forward is possible.

Containing without absorbing: the necessary balance

Helping another does not mean carrying their pain but being present without melting. In emotional solidarity, we must learn to care without neglecting ourselves. This implies sustaining listening, sharing resources, accompanying... but also knowing when to say, "I need a break" or "now it's my turn". In relational psychology, the concept of permeable boundaries is worked on a lot: being available but not invaded. Because a support network is not a place to fall beyond measure, but a fabric that allows no one to sink completely.

Shared strength: when one falls, the other holds.

Solidarity networks are not hierarchical structures where one saves and the other is saved. They are circles where the role changes according to the moment. Today you listen, tomorrow they listen to you. Today you cry, then you laugh with the one who cried with you. This cyclical dynamic creates genuine bonds where strength is not measured by how many times you fall, but by how many times you are picked up without demanding anything from you. In difficult times, knowing that you don't have to hold everything alone completely changes the experience of pain.

Because accompanying each other in the dark illuminates little by little

Sometimes we don't need solutions, motivational phrases, or recipes to feel better. Sometimes the only thing that heals is the presence of someone who dares to stay when everything looks gray. Not to get up, not to tell you that everything is going to be okay, but to sit next to you and say, "you're not alone." And that, although it seems simple, is one of the most powerful ways to save someone from the abyss.

Because when you're in your own storm, the last thing you need is someone from the shore shouting advice to you. What you need is someone who takes off their shoes, walks with you into the mud and says: "yes, this hurts, but I'm here". That silent company, without filters or expectations, is what sometimes keeps the flame burning when there is not much more left.

The human soul recognizes those who have passed through the same tunnels. Not much explanation is needed among those who have learned to breathe underwater. A gesture, a look, an "I believe you" can break internal walls that had been intact for years. Because true empathy doesn't seek to fix you, it seeks to sustain you while you rebuild yourself at your own pace.

In a culture where toxic optimism, "you can" at all costs, and the pressure to be "okay" twenty-four hours a day are rewarded, finding someone who won't be scared by your shadows is a sacred gift.

Someone who doesn't run away when you cry, who doesn't change the subject when you're broken, who doesn't get uncomfortable with your raw truth. That person not only accompanies you: it dignifies you.

And the most beautiful thing is that when two people accompany each other from that place, without the need to fake light when everything is dark, a flame is lit that does not depend on the environment. A flame that says: "if you endure, so do I". And little by little, even if the world doesn't change, even if the problem isn't erased, something inside you is rearranged. Because you're no longer struggling alone.

Real solidarity does not need speeches. It only needs presence. It doesn't require you to be well, it offers you a place to be bad without guilt. And in times where everyone runs for validation and applause, sitting down to share silence with someone who does not judge... it is pure medicine for the soul. A medicine that does not cure all at once, but it does make you want to continue. And that, sometimes, is all that is needed.

Celebrating Diversity: Recognizing Beauty in Differences

We live in a world that has taught us to fear what is different rather than admire it. From childhood, we are pushed towards the idea of "normality" as if it were a peak that we must all reach. But the truth is that this summit does not exist, it is a collective illusion that crushes identities, uniforms bodies, silences voices and turns authenticity into a risk. From the point of view of social psychology, diversity is not only inevitable, but necessary for collective well-being. Differences do not divide as they enrich. And acknowledging this is not a gesture of condescending tolerance, but a profound act of emotional justice.

What makes you weird, makes you real?

Diversity is not limited to skin color, sexual orientation, or religion. It also includes ways of thinking, ways of loving, lifestyles, emotional expressions, capacities, bodies, rhythms, accents, and silences. Every trait that makes you feel "out of the box" is also a point of uniqueness. Humanistic psychology reminds us that the meaning of life is not in fitting in, but in expressing oneself. And when you give yourself permission to be you, you're opening up space for others to breathe without fear, too. Your weirdness may be the emotional refuge that someone else was looking for.

Diversity is not disorder: it is harmony in movement.

Nature is diverse: no two leaves are the same, no two skies are identical, and no single way to bloom. And yet, everything works with unpredictable beauty. The same should happen with human beings. Thinking differently is not a threat; it is an opportunity. From the perspective of collective learning, sharing with those who are not like you expands your horizons, challenges your prejudices, and humanizes your gaze. Instead of asking "why are you like this?", we could start saying "how interesting that you are like this".

Difference doesn't need defense, it needs space.

Many people spend their lives asking permission to exist explaining their way of dressing, justifying their identity, softening their personality so as not to make them uncomfortable. But diversity doesn't need explanation, it needs acceptance. In affirmative therapy, we work on just that: stop defending what simply is. We didn't come into the world to convince anyone that we deserve respect, but to take our place unapologetically for not meeting the standard roster.

Celebrate, not just accept.

Accepting diversity is the minimum. Celebrating it is the real change. It is not enough to "tolerate" what is different, like someone who endures annoying noise. It is about recognizing that differences make the world a richer, wiser, more humane place. And that every time someone dares to live out loud their authenticity, they are lighting the way for others to also let go of fear. Celebration does not require understanding everything, but being willing to open one's eyes and put aside the ego that believes it has the only truth.

Because the soul is not measured in labels, but in freedom.

True beauty is in the nuances, in the contrasts, in the mixture, in what does not fit together. To love diversity is to love life in all its forms. And when we begin to look at each other without looking for reflection, but for encounter, we stop being afraid of what we do not understand... and we begin to learn from it.

Because in a world where many want you to look like everyone else, being yourself — and respecting others are also — is the most revolutionary, most empathetic, and beautiful act you can choose.

Holistic Wellness: The Benefits Of Authenticity In Mental, Emotional, And Physical Health

Being yourself is not only liberating... It's also healthy. Literally. Authenticity, understood as the coherence between what you feel, think, say, and do, is one of the most solid foundations of integral well-being. From clinical psychology to psychosomatic medicine, studies agree that living disconnected from your truth generates deep wear and tear: anxiety, fatigue, chronic sadness, digestive disorders, insomnia, and even physical pain with no apparent explanation. It's not magic, it's biology: pretending to be tired, repressing sick people, and lying to oneself has side effects. On the other hand, when you live in tune with yourself, your body notices it, your mind appreciates it, and your nervous system finally lets its guard down.

Mental health: less internal conflict, more emotional clarity

Living authentically reduces mental noise. You don't have to remember which version of yourself you showed, or act on what others expect. From cognitive therapy, authenticity reduces cognitive dissonance: that short circuit between what you think and what you do. When that conflict disappears, your mind feels clearer, your emotions less confusing and your self-esteem more stable. You don't need to put on a mask every time you go out anymore, because the face you show looks a lot like the one you have inside. And that coherence, although it seems simple, is an enormous emotional break.

Emotional Health: Less Guilt, More Self-Compassion

Being authentic also involves acknowledging your emotions without judging them. You no longer need to disguise anger as sarcasm, sadness as busyness, or joy as modesty. You can feel uncensored. Emotional psychology calls it emotional literacy: knowing what you feel, to know what you need. And when that happens, healthier self-regulation mechanisms are activated. Instead of exploding or swallowing everything, you learn to express yourself clearly. And when something changes you stop demanding perfection from yourself and start practicing compassion. You don't have to be the best version of yourself all the time... just an honest version.

Physical health: the body also breathes authenticity.

Although it may not seem like it, the body listens to everything you keep silent. When you live in constant tension to please, please or pretend, the nervous system is activated as if you are in constant danger. This produces cortisol in excess, alters sleep, lowers your defenses, and affects your digestion. Integrative medicine has proven it time and time again: sustained emotional stress generates physical symptoms. But when you start being you, your body stops fighting a borrowed identity and relaxes. You breathe easier. You sleep deeper. You eat with more awareness. Your posture changes. Your energy stabilizes. Because at last, all of you are aligned.

Healthier relationships: when you no longer need to translate.

Being authentic is not only a gift you give yourself. It's also an invitation for your relationships to breathe. Because when you stop pleasing out of obligation and begin to show yourself as you really are – with your lights, your entanglements, and your uncomfortable laughter – something is reordered: the false is filtered, and the real remains.

You stop wasting energy calculating every word or measuring your gestures as if you were in an eternal interview. And that, in addition to freeing you, clarifies the panorama. Those who were only there for the softened version of you begin to fade. And in their place, those who do not need you to act to want to stay appear.

Authentic relationships are less noisy, but much stronger. They argue without theater, laugh without pose and cry without shame. And it's not that there aren't conflicts, of course there are. But the difference is that, instead of exploding, they talk. Because when both sides show themselves as they are, there is no need to play emotional fortune tellers.

From the psychology of bonds, it is more than proven when two people allow themselves to be genuine, the bond becomes more durable, more resilient, and much more nurturing. Not only because they understand each other better, but because they feel more emotionally secure.

And best of all: the emotional peace that is gained is priceless. Sleeping peacefully, knowing that you don't have to maintain a character to sustain your relationships, is a form of well-being that is not sold in jars, but it is noticeable in the skin, in the spirit, in the soul.

So if you've ever wondered if it's worth, being you, even if that scares a few, the answer is simple: yes. Because for every door that closes for the sake of not pretending, a window opens with a view of real links. The kind that doesn't require you to wear costumes... only presence. And in a world of so much filtering, that's an emotional miracle.

Authenticity: the most powerful prescription that is not sold in pharmacies

Being authentic is not going through life shouting truths like bullets or turning every conversation into a dramatic confession. It is not a matter of exhibiting everything, but of not hiding the essential. Being authentic is when you stop asking the world for permission to be you. It is when you decide that your peace is worth more than the approval of others, and that your truth – no matter how uncomfortable, strange, or changing it may be – deserves to be heard, starting with you.

Authenticity is not only a beautiful value to write on social networks or tattoo on your forearm. It is a mental health tool. When you start living coherently, when you stop acting like you're a supporting character in your own story, the body appreciates it. Anxiety goes down, insomnia calms down, you breathe deeper, your stomach doesn't twist as much anymore. Because pretending is tiring but lying to yourself... Sick.

Being you without costumes is like taking off a tight shoe at the end of the day. You didn't know how much it hurt until you felt relief. Authenticity at first is scary, yes. You feel exposed, fragile, weird. But then, when you see that the world doesn't end because you stop pleasing, the good stuff begins. You start choosing what you do, what you don't, what you do now, what you never do again. Your energy is no longer wasted on holding masks. Your bonds are cleaned up. Your words weigh differently.

And be careful, being authentic does not mean being enlightened or having everything clear. On the contrary, many times to be authentic, that is: "I don't know who I am exactly, but at least I don't want to continue betraying myself". It is giving yourself permission to be contradictory, to change your mind, to feel a lot or not to feel anything, but without judging yourself for it. It's looking in the mirror and, even if you don't love everything you see, knowing that at least you're seeing someone real.

In a world that applauds appearance and penalizes difference, being unapologetically is revolutionary. It is pure medicine. It has no side effects, but it does have a great side effect: freedom. And when you live from that place, you don't just heal... You also invite others to take off their costumes, to turn down the volume on fear, and to remind themselves that we didn't come to pretend. We came to live. And living, really, begins when you dare to be who you are, without anesthesia.

Genuine Relationships: The Depth Of Bonds When They Are Grounded In Truth

The deepest relationships are not built with perfection, but with truth. They do not arise from seeming nice, or agreeing on everything, or hiding the parts that we think the other will not accept. They are born when we let our guard down and dare to be who we really are, with our lights, shadows, wounds, fears, contradictions, and manias. From the psychology of authentic bonds, true connection occurs when both people relate from being, not from what should be. There is no game of appearances, nor tacit pacts of "I pretend and so do you". There is honesty. And although that is uncomfortable at first, it creates much more solid and human bonds.

Less façade, more presence

When you don't need to impress, you can be really present. You're no longer thinking about how to sound more interesting, or calculating whether what you said was too much, or afraid of appearing fragile. You can just be. That completely changes the quality of the relationship: you go from emotional performance to real intimacy. From couples therapy and conscious bonds, it is observed that the healthiest relationships are not those that have fewer conflicts, but those that have the most capacity to be honest without destroying themselves. And that's only possible when you both feel like you don't need to hide.

Trust is not born from the beautiful, but from the consistent

Showing yourself as you can be scary, but it also allows you to build a kind of confidence that you don't get with fake smiles. Because when someone sees you cry, get angry, make a mistake, or confess a fear and still stays, you understand that that bond has roots. Relationships based on truth are less perfect, yes, but much more resilient. There is not so much to explain or justify anymore: there is a silent emotional language that says, "I see you, I understand you, you don't need to act with me".

Shared vulnerability: the cement of real links

Being vulnerable is not an act of weakness, but of emotional courage. And when two people allow themselves to share from that place, the bond becomes deeper. There are no longer just words: there is harmony. From humanistic psychology, this openness creates a space of resonance where the other is not an observer, but a companion on the road. And in that field, there is something that does not happen in superficial relationships: the possibility of healing. Because when someone validates you from experience and not from judgment, something inside you relaxes and begins to trust that you are no longer alone.

Relationships that nurture, not exhaust

Genuine connections don't feel like an obligation or a constant struggle to maintain them. They feel like they are breaking. Not because everything is perfect, but because everything is real. Instead of leaving a conversation feeling exhausted or confused, you leave feeling seen. Understood. Sometimes even more you than before. In psychotherapy, this is called emotional regulation: the presence of the other helps regulate your internal world. And that is not achieved by bonds based on appearance, but those that are made of real raw, but shared.

Because when the relationship is genuine, you don't need acting: you need presence.

Lying seduces because it is comfortable. It accommodates you in an edited story, with rehearsed dialogues and provisionally happy endings. But the truth, as uncomfortable as it is, has roots. It does not evaporate when circumstances change, it does not break at the first conflict, it does not need spelling checks before leaving. Truth does not embellish it sustains. And in a world full of cardboard relationships, where everything is fast, aesthetic and perfectly publishable, finding a bond where you can take off your armor is like finding water in the middle of an emotional desert.

A real relationship doesn't always look good in photos. Sometimes it looks like an early morning conversation where they are both exhausted but decide not to give up. Or as an awkward silence that no one tries to fill with cheap phrases. He sees himself as two people who allow themselves to be weird, fragile, intense, contradictory. Who look without make-up of the soul and, even so, choose to stay. That is not built with filters, it is built with truth. And that truth, even if it hurts, even if it brings out the worst before showing the best, is the foundation of everything that is worthwhile.

Because the most beautiful relationships are not the ones that seem eternal from the first date, but the ones that survive the first collapse without losing respect. Those that reinvent themselves without betraying their essence. Those who are not afraid to show scars, or admit that they are sometimes afraid, or confess that not everything is clear... but even so they are still there, clinging to honesty as their only compass.

In times where what you appear is valued more than what you really are, being able to love and be loved without acting, without rehearsing, without having to earn points for good behavior, is revolutionary. And profoundly healing. Because when someone loves you without you having to lie to yourself to deserve it, you discover something powerful: you don't need to be perfect to be worthy of love. You just need to be you. And find someone who dares to do the same.

In the end, the real thing is not perfect. But the perfect is not true either. And between the two, what feels alive, even if it hurts sometimes, will always be better than what looks beautiful, but it is empty inside. Because in the imperfect that is built with truth... That's where love really dwells. No filter. No script. Fearless.

The Power of Vulnerability: How Opening Up Strengthens Human Connections

In a culture that rewards self-reliance, composure, and impeccable image, being vulnerable seems crazy. But from emotional psychology, vulnerability is not a defect that must be corrected, but a powerful tool to create authentic bonds. Opening up does not mean overflowing without measure but showing oneself without masks. And while that is scary—because it means the risk of being hurt, misunderstood, or rejected, it's also the only way to experience a deep human connection. Because no one can absolutely love you if they never see you truly.

Being brave is not being afraid: it is opening up in spite of it.

Being vulnerable involves saying "I'm scared", "I don't know what to do", "this hurts me", "I need help". And that, in a society that applauds emotional control as if it were maturity, feels like a leap without a net. But that's exactly where the magic begins. In therapy it is seen daily: people who allow themselves to show themselves as they are, even in their most clumsy or broken moments, generate greater empathy and trust in their relationships. Because when one opens up, he's saying to the other, "I trust you're not going to use this against me." And that creates an intimacy that no superficial conversation can achieve.

Being imperfect invites the other to do the same.

Vulnerability is contagious — in the best sense. When someone dares to speak from the heart, without poses or armor, they give the other person permission to take off their costume as well. What starts as an awkward confession can end up in a liberating conversation. From the psychology of therapeutic groups and communities, this is called emotional modeling: a person who opens up emotionally generates a mirror effect in those around them. And in that reflection the real connection is born, not from the character, but from the soul.

Vulnerability is not weakness: it is emotional awareness in its purest form.

There's a big difference between being vulnerable and being dependent, dramatic, or unstable. Opening up doesn't mean letting go of everything without a filter or waiting for the other to save you. It means speaking from your center, honestly, to connect, not to manipulate. It is the act of saying "this is what I feel" without demanding anything in return. And when you achieve that, you begin to relate from a more mature, more conscious, more present place. Integrative therapy insists that there is no emotional health without vulnerability: the opposite is anesthesia, and emotional anesthesia may seem functional... but it kills the connection.

Opening up also heals the body: it is not just a matter of the soul.

Emotions that are not expressed do not disappear: they accumulate in the body. The tension of pretending, the effort to always appear good, the weight of keeping quiet about what hurts, all of this manifests itself in the form of insomnia, muscle aches, anxiety, constant fatigue. But when you speak from the truth, even in a trembling voice, you are releasing a burden. It is no coincidence that many people cry in relief after saying something they had been keeping for years. It's the body letting go of the weight. And sometimes, that vulnerable first step is more healing than any pill.

Human connection: what happens when someone looks at you and doesn't run away from you.

There are few things more healing than showing yourself vulnerable and, instead of rejection, receiving a hug. That instant in which you dare to say, "this is what I am, with everything and everything" and the other person not only does not run away but stays... it marks a before and after. It is as if the soul released the air, it had been holding for years.

Because that's where what life was hurting begins to heal: the shame of not feeling enough, the fear of abandonment for not being "what is expected", the judgment that you learned to throw at yourself before others did. To show yourself in the flesh and not be punished for it... That does reconfigure anyone's emotional history.

And the fact is that true love, the one that is truly worthwhile, is not conquered or forced. You don't negotiate or win on merit. It comes when you let your guard down. When you're no longer acting or asking forgiveness for existing as you are. And if he remains after seeing you like this, without shield or pose, then yes: it is good love.

From there, everything changes. Because you no longer need to be the strongest, funniest, or most successful version to feel worthy of affection. You can cry, fail, feel lost... and still deserve company. And no one can take that certainty away from you. It's your emotional anchor when the world outside gets rough.

And something curious happens: the more we remove the filters, the more we connect. Not from the character, but from the human. Because no one falls in love with the emotional makeup we use to fit in. We fall in love with what beats underneath. Of spontaneous laughter, of comfortable silence, of the gaze that does not judge.

So, if you're thinking of continuing to hide so that they want you, stop. Because when you finally dare to be without asking permission, you find bonds where you don't have to negotiate your existence. And there, right there, that unconditional love is born. The one who doesn't ask you to be perfect... just that you are. And that, although it may not seem like much, is everything.

Inspiring Others: How Your Authenticity Can Open Paths for Those Who Come After

Being yourself is not only a personal act of liberation, but also a public declaration of possibilities. Every time you choose to show yourself as you are, without hiding your emotions, your differences, or your history, you are doing something much bigger than defending your identity: you are opening a door for others to also be encouraged to cross it. From social and developmental psychology, it is known that authentic behaviors have a powerful modeling effect. That is, when someone sees you choose you over fear, they begin to wonder if they could also do the same.

Your story can be someone else's map.

Maybe you're just trying to survive, to find your voice, to rebuild yourself from who you are. But without realizing it, your process is serving as a reference for someone else who still doesn't dare.

When you share what you felt, what you doubted, what you lost, and what you chose, you are giving away light. Narrative psychology shows that well-told personal stories not only inspire, but they also repair. Because when someone else hears that someone like him made it, a new inner belief is activated: maybe I can too.

Courage is contagious: you dare, and someone else breaks free.

There is nothing more powerful than seeing someone being consistent with themselves, even if it costs them comfort. That courage has an expansive effect. Sometimes you don't even need to speak just your presence, your way of walking, your way of saying "this is who I am, and I don't apologize for it". From the psychology of emotional leadership, the referents are not those who have the most followers, but those who live in tune with their truth. And you, by living from your authenticity, become a silent reference for those who are looking for a way out of the labyrinth.

Even your mistakes inspire me if you go through them with truth.

Highlighting your achievements is easy; showing your falls and still standing, that has an impact. People don't connect with your perfection, but with your humanity. And when you show yourself in process, without pretensions of having everything resolved, you are teaching something much more valuable than success: you are teaching the way. From the psychology of resilience, the story of overcoming is valued more than that of victory. Because the first motivates, and the second sometimes only intimidates. Being authentic, even in your most vulnerable moments, doesn't detract from your value: it makes you real. And that does leave a mark.

Breaking the mold is making room for those who come.

Your authenticity also serves a collective function. Questioning what is imposed, making what has been silenced visible, opening uncomfortable conversations... All of this not only improves your life, but it also improves the world for those who cannot yet speak. From an ethical and social perspective, choosing to be you out loud is also an act of generosity. Because if you do it, someone else will understand that it's not wrong to be different, that you're not broken, that you're not alone. Your freedom opens the way. Your voice legitimizes other voices. Your presence, such as it is, can be the refuge that another does not yet find in himself.

Because being you is not only for you: it is also for those who still do not dare.

Every time you choose not to hide, you are planting something. Sometimes it will be admiration, other times it will be discomfort. But it will always be an invitation: to look differently, to live more freely, to break the mold, to choose from within. Don't underestimate the power of your authenticity. Not everyone will applaud, but many will remember you as the one who lit the spark. And if just one person dares to start their own path thanks to yours, it will be worth it.

Because sometimes, inspiring is not doing great things. It's simply daring to be. And do it out loud.

Make it clear: Revolution starts with your voice.

In a world where so many people speak, shout, give their opinions and publish, it seems that raising your voice is just making more noise. But no. Raising your voice for acceptance and diversity is not making a scandal, it is making space. That is to say, "here I am" in a system that has so many times told us "better shut up". And yes, sometimes it makes you uncomfortable. But what really bothers me is not the sound, but the truth behind that sound. Because accepting diversity is not applauding what is "different" as if it were a circus number. It is to understand that there is no right mold to be human.

Quiet you look more... Oppressed.

We have been taught that talking about certain things is bad taste. That the personal is not said out loud. That the different should stay at home or put on makeup so that it does not scare. But what is not named, does not exist. And what does not exist, is not defended. Therefore, raising one's voice is an act of existence. Because when you dare to say what you are, what you think, what you dream and what you are no longer going to allow, something changes. Maybe not the whole world, but the square meter that surrounds you. And that, believe me, is more revolutionary than any political speech.

Your authenticity is not noise: it is a necessary frequency.

Being yourself out loud doesn't mean giving speeches with a sad violin background. Sometimes it's just saying "no" without apology, dressing how you want, loving as you are born or daring to occupy a space without feeling like you're stealing air. That is already emotional activism. Because your existence as it is—without editing, without filter, and without permission—is telling the world that you can live without pretending. And the best thing: he is giving permission to others who are not yet encouraged. You're the microphone on that someone else needed to start singing their own song.

Sometimes, raising your voice is also raising your eyebrow.

Striving for acceptance and diversity doesn't mean walking around with banners 24/7 (although if you do, don't be short of SHINE). Sometimes it is enough to question a joke that is not laughable, to point out an injustice that everyone ignores, to correct the guy who continues to believe that "that's a fashion". Because every time you speak, you're sowing an uncomfortable seed. And yes, it may not grow right away. But sooner or later, someone is going to sit on it and realize that diversity does not bite, diversity liberates.

You're not alone: others are waiting for you to start to follow you.

Sometimes we think that we are the only weird, different ones, sensitive ones, "intense" ones. But believe me: there are lots of people feeling outside the system, waiting for someone to say what they still don't dare. Raising your voice is not shouting to be heard. It is speaking so that others remember that they also have throats. It's turning on the light so that no one else has to dress in the darkness of guilt or shame.

And if you're going to make noise, let it be the good one.

Acceptance and diversity are not fashion topics or campaign slogans. They are human rights, basic emotions, social structures that can no longer be optional. So yes, make noise. But do it with intention, with humor, with truth and with that authenticity that sometimes annoys, but always illuminates.

Because in the end, it's not about the world applauding you. It's about that, when you speak, you listen to yourself. And say without fear: this is me, this is me, this is me... and I don't intend to apologize for existing like this.

A future with more open doors: the vision of a world where difference is celebrated, not punished.

Imagine a world where they don't apologize to you before telling you who they are, where no one has to rehearse their personal story as if it were a job interview, where doors aren't locked but decorated with signs that say, "Come in, you fit in here." Such a world is not utopia... it is debt. Because the truth is, until now, many have been taught to bend down to pass through doors that were designed for minuscule identities. And that, even if it is disguised as tradition or morality, is violence with a bow.

What if difference was not tolerated, but applauded?

Tolerance is only the first step. It's like saying "I'll let you be here, but don't make too much noise". On the other hand, celebrating difference is something else: it is inviting her to the table, giving her space, learning from her, laughing with her codes, letting her paint the world with colors that you didn't know existed. From the psychological and human point of view, living in diversity is not a favor that is done to the "others"; it is a gift that one gives to oneself. Because every time you open up to what is different, your world expands, your ego is loosened, and prejudices are uninstalled as if they were applications that are no longer useful.

The future is not built with mold, but with new materials.

If we keep repeating old formulas, we're just going to reproduce the same exclusions with better filters. A world with more open doors implies redesigning how we educate, how we love, how we hire, how we listen. It means to stop asking "why are you like this?" and start saying "it's good that you are like this". It involves creating environments where no one has to ask permission to exist, or explanations to be. Because weird isn't weird: it's just something you haven't understood yet... And that, by the way, is not the fault of the other.

That labels do not replace invitations.

It's not about pigeonholing everyone with a new inclusive label. It is about understanding that each human being is more than an acronym, a flag, or a box on a form. In that future with more open doors, what is celebrated is not only identity, but the story behind it. The courage of those who dared to show themselves, the patience of those who continue to explain, and the laughter shared between those who were nothing alike, but decided to build something together, are celebrated.

Difference is not a threat, it is medicine.

In a world where so many continue to compete to be right, difference reminds us that there is no single way to live, feel or be. That we can coexist without cloning each other. That we can dissent without saying goodbye. That we can build bridges with wood of a different color. Diversity is not disorder:

it arranges the pieces so that no one is left out of the game.

And if the future is open, let it be so in style.

An absolutely free future will not be silent or monochromatic. It will be loud, vibrant, sometimes uncomfortable, and many times unpredictable. But it will be fairer. More human. And not because we are all the same, but because we will finally have understood that this was never necessary to live together.

Because celebrating difference is not just about opening a door... it is removing the lock from fear. And to make the world a place where everyone can enter dancing, even if they do it at the wrong time.

Reminder: Living Behind Open Doors Is A Process, Not A Destiny

No one wakes up one bright day, throws the keys out of the window and shouts "from today I live with an open soul!". Hopefully. But the truth is, living behind open doors isn't an epic fireworks event... It is a daily process, sometimes uncomfortable, often confusing, and almost always full of mini victories that only one notices. It is about opening internal locks that have been rusting for years due to fear, judgment, or habit. It's not a goal that is achieved with a certificate, but a constant practice that begins every time you decide not to hide.

One day you dare to say what you think. Another, no. And it's okay.

There are days when you feel free, strong, and even think you could give a TED talk about authenticity. And next, you cringe again in front of someone else's gaze or shut up to avoid trouble. That doesn't make you a hypocrite. It makes you human. Because living with an open heart does not mean ever again being afraid but learning to walk with that fear without letting it close again. From the psychology of growth, the important thing is not how many times you doubt, but how many times you choose yourself, even if it is with a trembling voice.

Not all doors open suddenly... some need oil, time, and therapy.

There are old wounds that are not resolved with beautiful statements or cup phrases. They require inner work, patience, sometimes professional help, and many times letting go of the idea that you should "go faster." Every door you decide to open confronts you with parts of yourself that you may have left in the emotional basement. And that is tiring. But it also liberates. The process of living in openness is like an emotional move: messy, full of things you didn't know you were still carrying, but also full of surprises that remind you how much you've grown.

Living behind open doors does not mean letting just anyone in

Don't confuse openness with lack of limits. Opening up to the world doesn't mean letting everyone in with dirty shoes and toxic opinions. It means consciously choosing what you share, with whom and when. Authentic openness is not excessive exposure; it is voluntary intimacy. And that, more than vulnerability, is emotional wisdom. You decide who crosses, who watches from the outside and who doesn't even ring the doorbell.

Every attempt counts, even the ones that seem unsuccessful.

You showed your true opinion and were ignored. You spoke from the heart, and they didn't understand you. You dared to be you... and they criticized you. And? Does it mean it wasn't worth it? Not at all. Every time you choose to open up, even if the result is not ideal, you strengthen your emotional muscles. You are practicing coherence, courage, and fidelity to your own story. And although it sometimes hurts, it always leaves a mark. Above all, in you.

So breathing is not a race, it's a way of inhabiting yourself.

Being yourself is not an achievement, it is a daily act. Living behind open doors doesn't mean you'll never be afraid again that you're not going to stagger, or that you're over it all. It means that you choose to stop hiding, even when you fear what they might see. It's getting up in the morning and, with all your contradictions on your back, telling yourself: "even with all this, I'm still me... and that's fine."

Coming back to you doesn't always feel epic. Sometimes it's tiring. Sometimes you don't even know what part of you is coming back. But you choose to do it anyway, because you've already tasted what it feels like to live with the door closed and you don't want to go back there. You learned that hiding may protect you for a while, but it also locks you in. And that opening up, even if it hurts, allows you to really breathe.

You're going to have days when it's hard for you. Days where you doubt yourself, where you feel ridiculous for having shown so much, where you miss how comfortable it was to pretend. But the difference now is that you know how to recognize when you're shutting down. And you also know that you don't have to stay there. Because you have already learned the way back to your truth, even if sometimes you crawl through it.

There is no prize for this. There is no trophy for authenticity, nor ovation for emotional courage. There is something much quieter, but more valuable: peace. That lukewarm peace that appears when you stop negotiating with yourself to please others. That feeling of coherence that sets in when your inside and your outside finally coincide.

And you don't need everyone to understand you. Nor do they applaud you. Or that they follow you. You just need to keep walking with the certainty that your truth, though rare, hurt, or changing, is still valid. Because you're not here to fit in. You are here to live in.

So, if today you feel that you are more closed than usual, do not judge yourself. Breathe. Rest. And remind yourself that that door can open again. That you already know how. That you're not starting from scratch. You're coming back to yourself. One more time. And with more and more truth.

Reaffirmation: Authenticity as the Greatest Act of Self-Love and Resilience

Being you in a world that asks you every day to be something else is, without a doubt, a revolutionary act. Not a revolution with banners or speeches on a megaphone (although that is also the case), but an intimate revolution, silent at times, but powerful. Choosing your truth over easy acceptance, your path over the expectations of others, your voice over the collective noise is a way of saying in your ear: I respect you enough not to betray you. And that, in times when pretending seems more comfortable, is self-love in its purest and most ferocious version.

It's not just loving you; it's stopping abandoning yourself.

Authenticity is not about "loving yourself" as the wellness industry repeats between herbal teas and aromatic pillows. It's about stopping betraying yourself to fit in. Of not putting makeup on your soul to please everyone. To talk, even if you tremble, to say no, even if you feel guilty, to stay, even if they want to move you and to leave, even if they ask you to stay. To love your authenticity is to take care of yourself as you take care of the most fragile: with firmness, with tenderness, with presence.

Resist without raising your fist, but without bowing your head.

Being authentic is also endurance. Because when you refuse to mold yourself by the rules of what is acceptable, you are challenging the system without having to fight. You're saying: I don't need your permission to exist like this. And yes, that makes you uncomfortable. Sometimes annoying. But it also transforms. Because every time someone shows himself without apologizing, he opens a hole to the collective lie that we should all be equal. Your authenticity doesn't just defend you: it defends everyone's right to be diverse, imperfect, and deeply real.

Loving you like this, without subtitles or makeup, is not ego... It's integrity.

Accepting your contradictions, your slow processes, your emotional intensity, your strange ideas, your changes of route, your uncomfortable silences, is a way of inhabiting yourself without shame. And that, in a world that requires you to be stable, efficient, and decorative, is emotional resistance. You don't need to be perfect to be worthy. You don't need to be healed to be complete. You just need to stop editing for fear of making yourself uncomfortable.

Your authenticity shapes the space for those who are not yet encouraged.

When you choose not to hide, you not only do yourself good: you also become a reference for others. People who watch you from afar and think "if she can, if he dares, maybe I too". You won't always know. They won't thank you in front of you. But your simple presence, true to yourself, is already a luminous crack in the wall of collective pretense.

Because to be you, without apologizing, without asking permission, without measuring the impact, is to absolutely love yourself.

And when you love yourself like this, not from the mirror or from the likes, but from the roots, you begin to live from a place where you don't need applause to validate your existence. Authenticity is the most radical act of self-love because it does not seek to adorn you, but to honor you. And it's the deepest act of resistance because, even knowing that being you can cost you, you decide that there's nothing more expensive than getting lost.

So yes, reaffirm yourself. Every day. Even if you tremble. Even if they don't understand. Even if it bothers you. Because the world doesn't need any more educated copies. You need more people who dare to be what they are... without turning down the volume. And you, being you, are already changing the rules of the game.

For the end of the book, but never for the end of the road

Dear reader, dear reader, dear brave soul who has come this far:

If you are reading these lines, it may be because in some corners of your history there are wounds that are not always seen, silences that weigh more than screams, or battles that you fight alone, sometimes even against yourself. This letter is for you. For those who have been called "different" with the same intention with which others throw stones. For those who have felt in a room full of people and, even so, completely alone. For those who have grown tired of explaining why they don't fit in, why they don't obey, why they don't bow their heads.

This card is for you who are gay and have learned to read looks before reading words. For you who hid for so many years for fear of losing the love of those who claimed to love you. Let me tell you something clear, direct and from the soul: there is nothing to heal in you. Your identity is not a mistake; it is an act of courage. Your desire is not a deviation; it is a beautiful way of feeling. Your existence doesn't need permission. Take a deep breath and remember you are not alone. You are part of a lineage of people who broke the mold to build a more dignified world.

This letter is also for you, who, because of the color of your skin, your accent, your name, or your history, have been looked at with suspicion or treated as less. You are not the problem: racism is. And even if they want to convince you that you exaggerate, that it's just a joke, that "that's life", don't shut up. Because every time you name injustice, you are dismantling an old structure. Don't adapt to a society that asks you to shrink. Expand. Occupy the space that rightfully belongs to you. You are inheritance, strength, and possibility.

And for you, who don't let yourself be dragged along by fashions, who don't think like everyone else, who don't applaud what doesn't convince you: thank you. You're not crazy. You're not problematic. You are necessary. In a world of copies, your free thought is an offering. He continues to question, he continues to choose differently, he continues to create new ways of inhabiting what others only imitate. Even if they call you a rebel, even if they want to tame you, remember that every revolution begins with someone who got tired of pretending.

To you, woman who raises her voice in a world that still expects you to smile and obey, I embrace you with all respect. You are giant. And even if some still feel uncomfortable with your power, let them be uncomfortable. You didn't come to please: you came to transform. Every time you speak, you are leading the way. Every time you don't let yourself shut up, you're rewriting a story that was previously told without you. Don't tone it down. Don't soften your truth. The world needs your roar as much as it needs your cuteness.

And for you, who do not agree with a government, with a system, with an authority that uses power to oppress, do not apologize for dissenting. You are not a traitor. You are not exaggerating. You are awakened consciousness. Raising one's voice in the face of injustice is not rebellion: it is dignity. History is full of people who were silenced for thinking differently. But it is also written by those who never stopped saying what they thought. Be one of them. Your voice is part of a truth that has not yet been fully spoken.

This letter is, in fact, an invitation. To continue. To resist. Take a deep breath when they want to push you into the mold. To remember that being you is your greatest form of protest, love, and freedom. There is no straight path to authenticity. There are days of doubt, fear, and tiredness. But there are also moments of clarity, of deep connection, of guiltless pride. And believe me: they are worth it.

So, whoever you are, wherever you are, with the story you carry, the scars you hide, and the dreams you still dare not say out loud... go on. Not because it's easy. But because it's real. And the real, at the end of the day, is the only thing that saves us.

With all my respect,

With all my hope,

and with the certainty that you, being you, are already changing the world:

Thank you for existing without asking forgiveness.

Thank you for not giving up.

Thank you for opening your door.

Here we are.

And here we are.

Together.

About The Author

Alina A. Rubi is a psychologist, writer and trainer who is passionate about the power of words and listening to transform lives. Over the years, she has dedicated her career to accompanying people in their processes of self-knowledge, emotional healing, and personal development, always from a warm, respectful, and deeply human perspective.

Graduated in Psychology, Alina specialized in working with family ties, interpersonal dynamics and patterns learned from childhood. Its integrative approach combines sound theory with a close, empathetic look at each person's unique experiences. She has worked in both individual consultation and workshops and group spaces, helping others understand the root of their emotional wounds, build healthy boundaries, and redefine the way they relate to themselves and others.

Alina passionately believes that psychology is not just a field of study, but a bridge to personal freedom. That is why she dedicates a good part of her time to writing, convinced that psychological knowledge should be available to everyone. Her accessible and thoughtful texts seek to offer clarity on often taboo topics such as family trauma, guilt, difficulty in saying "no" or the weight of invisible loyalties. His style combines professional rigor with simple and often humorous language, to help digest truths that may be uncomfortable but necessary.

In addition to her clinical practice and her facet as a writer, Alina has also participated in training programs for professionals and has collaborated in community projects focused on mental health. He is especially interested in prevention: teaching us to recognize harmful patterns before they are perpetuated from generation to generation. For her, breaking family cycles is not an act of betrayal, but the greatest possible sign of love: the conscious decision not to inherit the same pain to others.

A faithful defender of the power of listening, Alina believes that many wounds begin where no one could, or wanted, to truly listen. That is why in his consultation he gives room to all voices: even to the most hurt, angry, or embarrassed parts of each person. Its objective is that each one can reconcile with their history, signify it and live with more authenticity and peace.

Today, Alina Rubi continues to write, attend, teach, and learn. Her work is a testament to her deep conviction: that we all deserve to build a life in which we don't have to choose between loving others and respecting ourselves. Because for her, psychology is much more than a profession: it is a tool for each person to become the conscious and compassionate narrator of their own story.

www.ingramcontent.com/pod-product-compliance
Lightning Source LLC
LaVergne TN
LVHW090406210926
848480LV00002B/477
9798230218494